Awesome Skies

Claire Throp

Illustrated by
Nicole LaRue

OXFORD
UNIVERSITY PRESS

Contents

Lights in the Sky

The Northern Lights can look like clouds, curtains or rays.
They can be green, red, blue, purple and pink.

They appear high above the Earth.

They can blink, wave or dance across the sky.

The Northern Lights is an incredible display of colours and shapes in the sky. These amazing glowing patterns only appear in some parts of the world. They also only appear at certain times of the year. If you want to see the Northern Lights, you have to plan your trip very carefully.

So wrap up warm! We're heading to the North Pole ...

Where to Find the Lights

This is where you are most likely to see the Northern Lights.

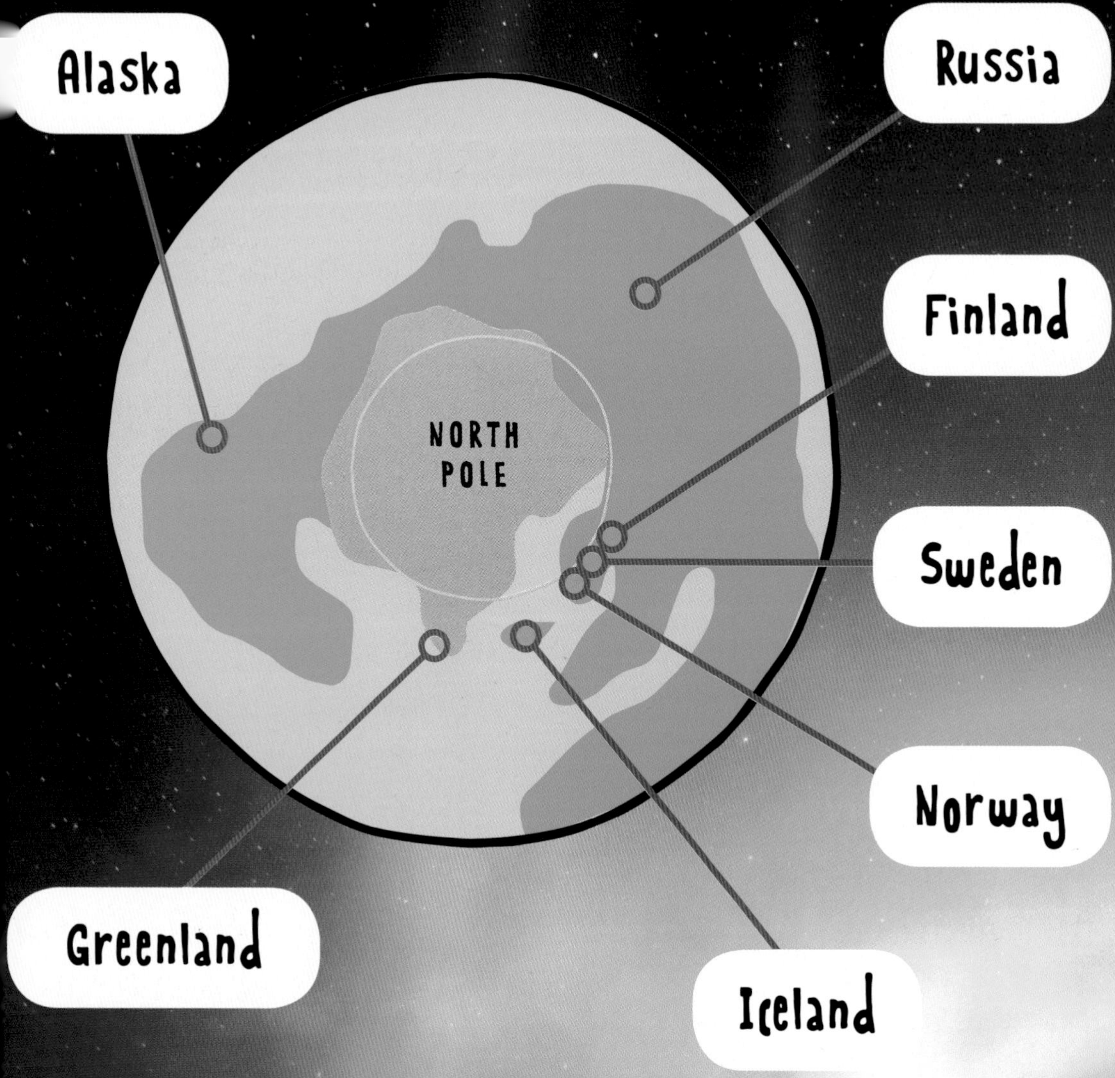

Alaska

Russia

Finland

NORTH POLE

Sweden

Norway

Greenland

Iceland

When the Northern Lights are in the sky near the North Pole, you can also see lights in the sky near the South Pole. These are called ... the Southern Lights!

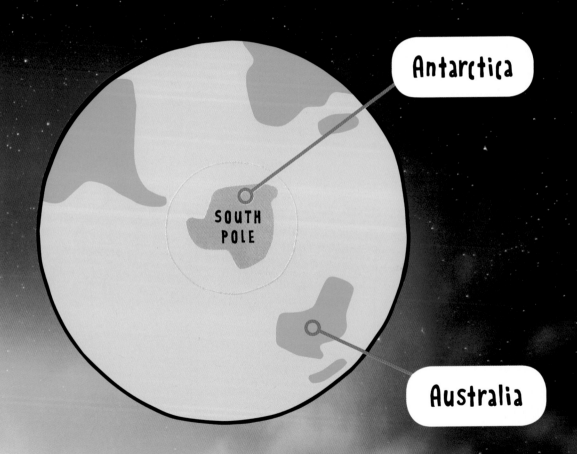

Antarctica

SOUTH POLE

Australia

Know Before You Go

The night sky needs to be very clear to see the Northern Lights. If it is cloudy, the view of the Lights is not as good.

When the Sun is active and fiery, the Northern Lights are bigger and better. Every 11 years the sun is very active, so the Northern Lights are very bright. 2014 was a great year to see the Northern Lights, so why not try and visit them in 2025?

Ellen went on a trip to see the Lights with her school.

Seeing the lights was so special.

When to visit the Northern Lights

Ellen was lucky. Many people travel a long way to look at the Lights and don't see anything at all! So when is the best time to go?

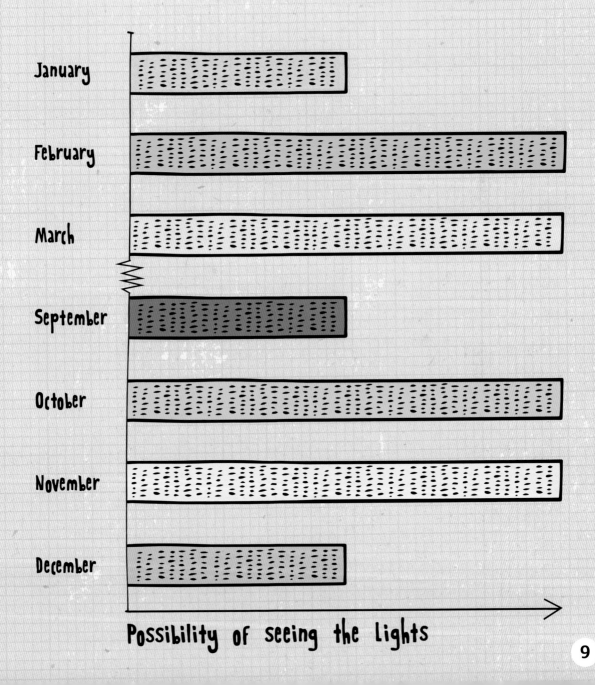

Possibility of seeing the lights

Get Set for an Adventure

If you want to see the Northern Lights, you need to plan ahead.

Be prepared to get cold!

We had to wait two hours in the sub-zero night air. It was freezing! The lights came at around 11 o'clock at night.

Don't forget to take these things:

- ✅ mittens
- ✅ hat
- ✅ camera
- ✅ binoculars

Get away from towns and cities.

We travelled a long way out of the city to avoid light pollution. The sky was clear so we had a wonderful view of the Milky Way. Then we saw the Northern Lights. They lit up the sky with waves of green light.

How are the Lights Created?

Let's go on an adventure which starts ... at the Sun!

1 Temperature
It's incredibly hot –
5000 degrees **Celsius.**

2 Storms
There are giant storms
all around you!

3 Solar flare
Suddenly a huge **solar
flare** sends you zooming
out into space.

4 Solar wind

You're now surfing on the **solar wind**, travelling at up to three million kilometres per hour!

5 Blue marble

In the distance you can see a blue marble, getting bigger and bigger. Hang on – it's the Earth!

6 North Pole

Now let's follow the solar wind down to the ground. When it reaches the Earth, it gets sucked down towards the North Pole like water going down a plug hole.

Making Colours

The next stop on your journey is the Earth's **atmosphere**.

7 The atmosphere

The Earth is surrounded by air – our atmosphere. The atmosphere is like an onion with lots of layers.

8 The thermosphere

The Lights are created in the layer called the **thermosphere**. This is between 80 and 400 kilometres above the Earth's surface.

Now it's time to make some colours!

9 Incredible colour

As you surf the solar wind down towards the surface of the Earth you see incredible colours all around you. You're in the middle of the Northern Lights!

Colour creation

The colours are created when the solar wind hits different gases in the atmosphere.

Red is created by **oxygen** high in the atmosphere.

Blues and **purples** are created by **nitrogen**.

Green is created by **oxygen** low in the atmosphere.

Making Myths

The Northern and Southern Lights have always been mysterious.

Before scientists understood what the Lights were, some people made up myths about them.

Myths are stories which were told long ago. They often explain unusual things that happen in the natural world.

In Finland, there are different myths which suggest that foxes cause the Northern Lights.

An Arctic fox is running through the mountains of the north. As it runs, its fur touches the mountains and sparks fly off into the sky. This is what makes the Northern Lights.

The fox's tail sweeps snow from the mountains up into the sky. This is what makes the Northern Lights.

Northern Lights Spotter Map

For hundreds of years, people from all around the world have told stories about the Northern Lights.

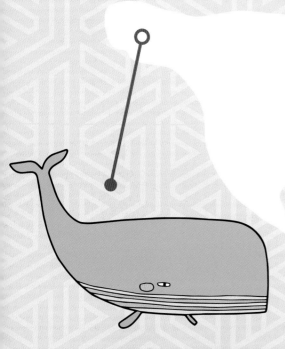

Alaska, USA

Tribes living along the Yukon River believed the glowing Lights were the **spirits** of deer, fish, seals and whales.

Wisconsin, USA

Inuit people believed the Lights were spirits who were using a walrus head as a football!

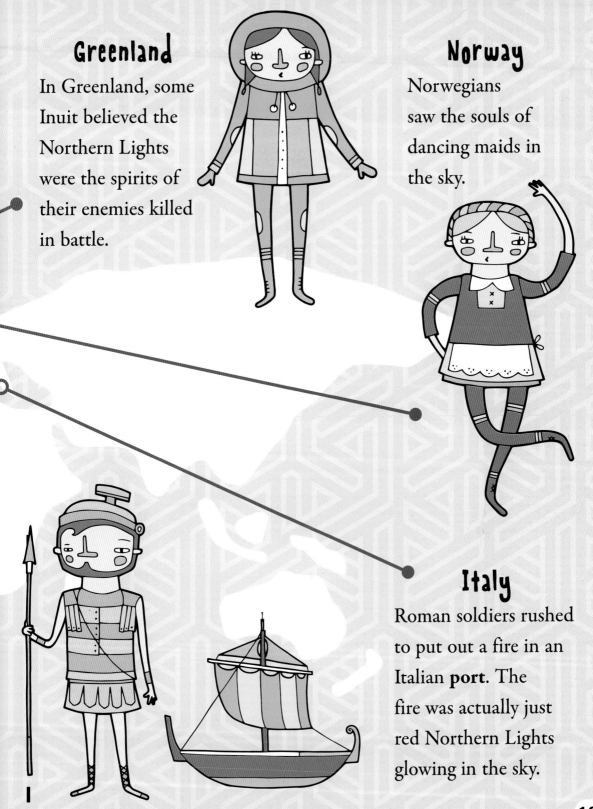

Greenland

In Greenland, some Inuit believed the Northern Lights were the spirits of their enemies killed in battle.

Norway

Norwegians saw the souls of dancing maids in the sky.

Italy

Roman soldiers rushed to put out a fire in an Italian **port**. The fire was actually just red Northern Lights glowing in the sky.

The Power of Nature

There is no way of knowing exactly when the Lights will appear. That is what makes it so exciting when they do!

One of my favourite parts of my trip to Iceland was seeing the Northern Lights.

It's all down to the sun, the weather and luck.

Now you know how these Lights are formed and where to see them. The closer you are to the North or South Poles, the brighter the Lights will be. But they've also been spotted in Scotland, Germany and Italy so you may not have to travel too far!

If the skies are clear, you could be lucky enough to see nature's most amazing light show. You just need to keep looking up.

Glossary

Arctic: from the regions around the North Pole

atmosphere: the gases around the Earth

Celsius: a scale used for measuring temperature

light pollution: when the sky is made brighter by man-made lights

Milky Way: a band of stars which makes a bright stripe across the night sky

nitrogen: a gas in the Earth's atmosphere

oxygen: a gas in the Earth's atmosphere

port: a waterside town or city where boats can tie up

solar flare: a sudden burst of energy from the Sun

solar wind: a stream of particles released from the Sun

spirits: souls

sub-zero: temperature below freezing

thermosphere: a layer of the atmosphere high above the Earth's surface where the Northern Lights are created

tribes: a group of people who live together and are ruled by a chief

Index

About the Author

I have been an editor and author for 11 years.
I like working at home because it means you
don't have to get up early! Of course, my cat
often has different ideas about me staying in bed late ...

I have wanted to see the Northern Lights for a long time.
So far I have been unlucky. I tried visiting Norway. Then
Iceland. Then Norway again. I even spent two months
travelling in Canada. Maybe I should try to see the
Southern Lights instead ...

Greg Foot, Series Editor

I've loved science ever since the day I took my papier mâché
volcano into school. I filled it with far too much baking
powder, vinegar and red food colouring, and WHOOSH! I
covered the classroom ceiling in red goo. Now I've got the best
job in the world: I present TV shows for the BBC, answer
kids' science questions on YouTube, and make huge explosions
on stage at festivals!

Working on TreeTops inFact has been great fun. There are so many
brilliant books, and guess what ... they're all packed full of awesome
facts! What's your favourite?